D0893657

I See Ovals

D.H. Dilkes

Bailey Books
an imprint of
Enslow Publishers, Inc.
40 Industrial Road
Box 398
Berkeley Heights, NJ 07922
USA

http://www.enslow.com

Bailey Books, an imprint of Enslow Publishers, Inc.

Copyright © 2011 by Enslow Publishers, Inc.

Library of Congress Cataloging-in-Publication Data

Dilkes, D. H.
  I see ovals / by D.H. Dilkes.
     p. cm. — (All about shapes)
  Includes index.
  Summary: "Simple text and photographs present a story with a theme about ovals"—Provided by publisher.
  ISBN 978-0-7660-3800-4
  1. Ovals—Juvenile literature. 2. Shapes—Juvenile literature. I. Title.
  QA483.D53 2011
  516'.152—dc22
                              2010018401

Paperback ISBN: 978-1-59845-151-1

Printed in the United States of America

052010 Lake Book Manufacturing, Inc., Melrose Park, IL

10 9 8 7 6 5 4 3 2 1

To Our Readers: We have done our best to make sure all Internet Addresses in this book were active and appropriate when we went to press. However, the author and the publisher have no control over and assume no liability for the material available on those Internet sites or on other Web sites they may link to. Any comments or suggestions can be sent by e-mail to comments@enslow.com or to the address on the back cover.

✪ Enslow Publishers, Inc., is committed to printing our books on recycled paper. The paper in every book contains 10% to 30% post-consumer waste (PCW). The cover board on the outside of each book contains 100% PCW. Our goal is to do our part to help young people and the environment too!

Photo Credits: Shutterstock.com

Cover Photo: Shutterstock.com

Note to Parents and Teachers

Help pre-readers get a jumpstart on reading. These lively stories introduce simple concepts with repetition of words and short simple sentences. Photos and illustrations fill the pages with color and effectively enhance the text. Free Educator Guides are available for this series at www.enslow.com. Search for the *All About Shapes* series name.

Contents

Words to Know

green

oval

I see ovals.

One I fly over.

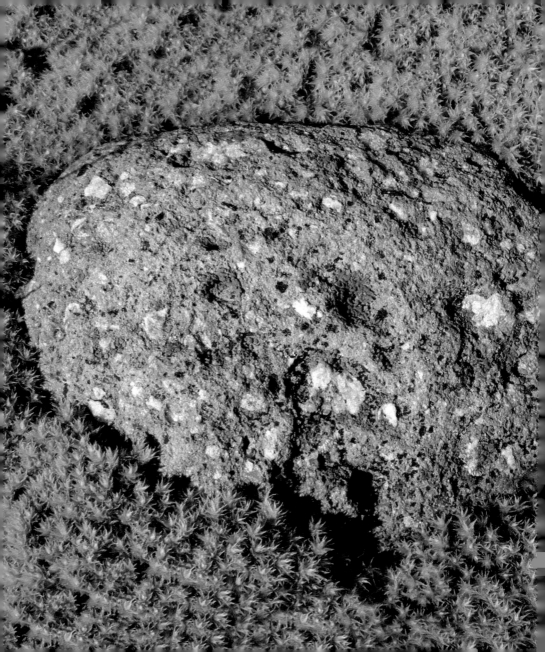

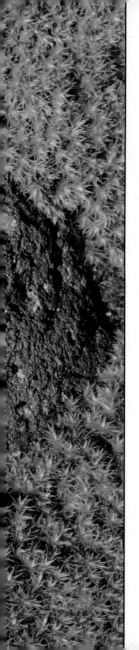

One to look under.

One made with my father.

An oval where I put
my drink

and one to walk on.

An oval can look pretty

or be the
color green.

Or help mother make

what I eat.